Seriously I   y
Rugby League

Dave Williams, age unknown, played rugby league from school age and progressed to open age rugby with St Patrick's in Leeds. In the late 1960s and early 1970s he played a few years of professional rugby league with Batley and later Bramley, alongside players such as Arthur Keegan, Graham Idle and Johnny Woolford until a serious knee injury in 1972 ended his playing days. So, as a keen photographer for many years, he took up photographing the sport he loved and had played. He  started getting work published in the early rugby league magazines, and that's how he and Sig met and teamed up in 2000 to start RLPhotos.com.

Sig Kasatkin, 57, is a freelance photographer specialising in rugby league and weddings. He was brought up in Castleford, supporting the team through its glory years of the Hardisty/Hepworth/Reilly era and for a long time took pictures of his team from the terraces. He started contributing to Harry Edgar's *Open Rugby* magazine in 1988 and 12 years later he and Dave Williams founded RLPhotos.com as a web-based rugby league agency to supply the press.

Gareth Walker, 29, is a freelance rugby league journalist working for the *People*, the *Guardian* and *Rugby League Express*. After being brought up watching Rochdale Hornets home and away, he first started writing for *League Express* at 16 and has continued ever since, being responsible for the paper's Championship coverage. He became the rugby league correspondent for the *People* on Grand Final night 2002, when Sean Long's last minute drop goal provided a dramatic first  night in the position. He began working for the *Guardian* in 2006, and continues to take a keen interest in Hornets' fortunes when work permits.

Seriously Funny Rugby League

Dave Williams and Sig Kasatkin
with Gareth Walker

VERTICAL EDITIONS

www.verticaleditions.com

First published in the United Kingdom in 2009 by Vertical Editions, Unit 4a, Snaygill Industrial Estate, Skipton, North Yorkshire BD23 2QR

www.verticaleditions.com

A CIP catalogue record for this book is available from the British Library

ISBN 978-1-904091-38-7

Cover design and typeset by HBA, York

Printed and bound by The MPG Books Group, Bodmin

CONTENTS

The authors are donating a portion of their royalties earned from this book to The Rugby Football League Benevolent Fund.

ACKNOWLEDGEMENTS

There are quite a few people who we would like to thank:

▶ Ace journalist Gareth Walker for his help with captions and his chapter introductions.

▶ England captain Jamie Peacock for taking time from his busy schedule to write his generous foreword.

▶ Fellow photographer John Rushworth for allowing us to use his 'kung fu' picture; the only picture in the book that neither of us took, but wish we had!

▶ Harry Edgar for getting us into this mess in the first place.

▶ All the players and officials, past and present, whose actions and expressions have provided the raw material for this book.

▶ Lastly, but certainly not least, thanks to both our wives Chris and Lynne for letting us cover rugby league instead of finding jobs around the house and taking them out every weekend!

These past 21 years have been fun—here's to many more, and we're already collecting images for the next book.

Cheers!

Dave and Sig

FOREWORD

The game of rugby league at international and club level is a tough sport played by athletes at the top of their fitness levels. Players lay their bodies on the line in every game with solid tackling and skilful ball handling. This creates spectacular images for the camera to capture. These rugby league players that entertain the fans week in and week out with their tackling, fitness and ball skills, also provide the game's photographers with unlimited action on the field. Some of this action is serious—hard running with crunching tackles as the players challenge each other endlessly throughout the game.

Despite rugby league's rock hard reputation, *Seriously Funny Rugby League* reveals that there are some lighter moments in the game. After 21 years photographing rugby league, Dave Williams and Sig Kasatkin reveal an alternative side of the sport through a selection of images they have taken over this time; players, officials and fans have not escaped their lenses.

We hope you enjoy this pictorial view of the funny, and more serious, moments in the great game of rugby league.

Jamie Peacock
Leeds Rhinos player
and England Captain

1
That's Not Rugby!

As with most professional sportsmen, today's Super League stars can often be found out on the golf course after a tough morning's training. But their sporting skills aren't just limited to fairways and greens—here we see some of the game's biggest names trying their hand at a whole host of other pastimes.

Blow football?

St Helens v Catalans Dragons 15 March 2008

Stacey Jones takes swimming lessons

Wakefield v Catalans Dragons, 11 March 2007

Summer rugby or swimming?

Huddersfield v St Helens, Paul Sculthorpe, 11 February 2005

Ready for the disciplinary punishment

Andrew Whitelam with his latest fly swatter, 9 August 2006

13

'Here's one way to beat the Aussies'

Sean Long, 9 August 2006

England coach Tony Smith studies the video evidence

23 June 2008

'Kung Fu Fighting'

Sam Obst shows his flying skills as he attempts to charge down Chris Thorman's kick, Huddersfield v Wakefield at Cardiff, 6 May 2007, photo courtesy of John Rushworth

'You're out!'

Danny Brough gets his sports mixed up, Wakefield v Castleford, Cardiff, 3 May 2008

'I can make a bunny rabbit shape with my torch and hands'

Jamie Benn, Castleford Tigers

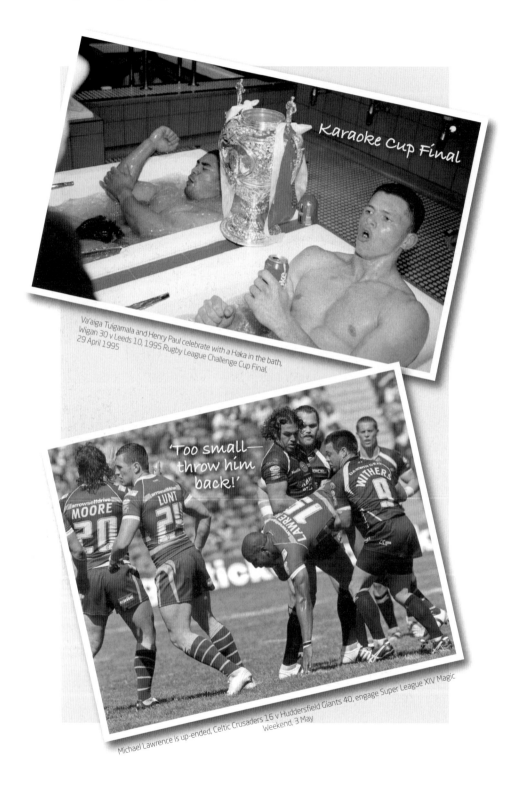

Karaoke Cup Final

Va'aiga Tuigamala and Henry Paul celebrate with a Haka in the bath,
Wigan 30 v Leeds 10, 1995 Rugby League Challenge Cup Final,
29 April 1995

'Too small—
throw him
back!'

Michael Lawrence is up-ended, Celtic Crusaders 16 v Huddersfield Giants 40, engage Super League XIV Magic
Weekend, 3 May

Chris Smith or
Tommy Cooper—
just like that!

York City Knights v Barrow Raiders. LHF Healthplan Division 2, 1 August 2004

'Glasshopper!'

Adrian Vowles takes up Tai Chi, Wakefield Trinity Wildcats v Bradford Bulls, 6 July 2003

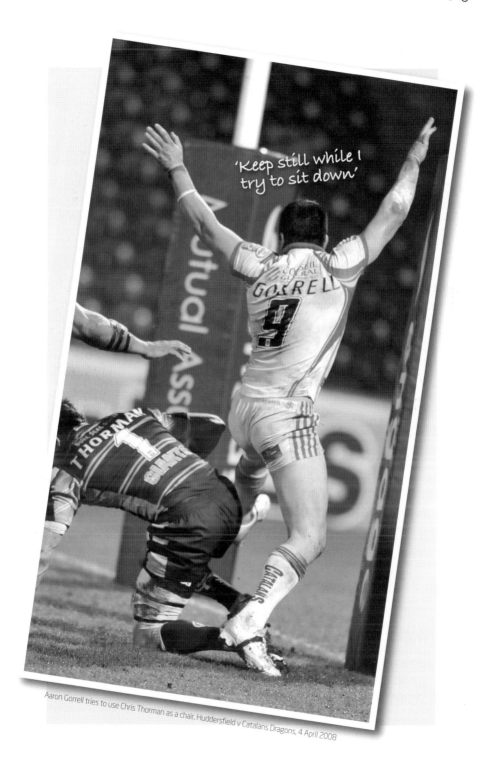

'Keep still while I try to sit down'

Aaron Gorrell tries to use Chris Thorman as a chair, Huddersfield v Catalans Dragons, 4 April 2008

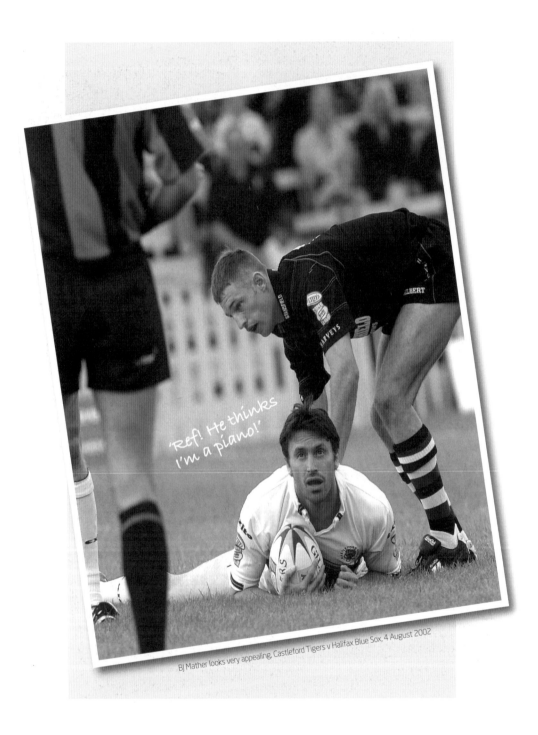

'Ref! He thinks I'm a piano!'

BJ Mather looks very appealing, Castleford Tigers v Halifax Blue Sox, 4 August 2002

'Please sir!'

Widnes' new signing Jonathan Davies is introduced to the crowd before the 1988 John Player Final Widnes v Wigan

Kevin Henderson tries the breast stroke

Wakefield Trinity Wildcats v Warrington Wolves, Super League XIII Round 10, 6 April 2008

Kevin Sinfield was
never one for the birds

18 February 2009

'Just like that!'

Rob Burrow does his Tommy Cooper impression, Great Britain v New Zealand, 1st Gillette Fusion Test, Galpharm Stadium, Huddersfield, 27 October 2007

Andy Johnson (London Broncos) takes up martial arts, Wakefield v London, 20 August 2000

Karl Fitzpatrick makes a great ironing board

Featherstone v Salford, 22 May 2008

'You're fired!'

Paul Dixon scores for Leeds, Leeds v Hull KR, 20 September 1992

31 May 2008

Danny McGuire returns from his stint in the Russian Army

'The invitation said smart casual'

Jamie Peacock looks a little under-dressed for this contest, 9 August 2006

2
What Not
To Wear

Fashion and rugby league players seem an unlikely combination—but the sport can throw up some eye-catching trends. Whether it's celebrating a famous victory or taking part in an unconventional promotion shoot, players can find themselves in some unusual poses. And, as our photographers have captured in this chapter, on-field clothing can also lead to some memorable images.

Bradford Northern buy their kit from a car boot sale

'Neil, what's your collar size?'

Neil Cowie has his collar felt by Sonny Nickle,
St Helens v Wigan in the 1993 Premiership
Final at Old Trafford, 16 May 1993

Richard Agar keeps
Sid Domic on a
tight lead

19 February 2006

The latest style in boots—Lee Crooks provides the pre-match entertainment

1989 Premiership Final, Old Trafford, 14 May 1989

Keiron Cunningham
was such a bonny
baby

26 August 2006

Paul Eastwood looks cool in his new hat

Great Britain v Australia 1st Test, Wembley, 27 October 1990

Laurie Daley admires Darryl Powell's shirt

Second Test between Great Britain and Australia, Old Trafford, 10 November 1990

Why do players insist on wearing trophies?

Nathan Graham, Dewsbury v Leigh, NFP Grand Final, 29 July 2000

Paul Deacon in
party mood

World Club Challenge, Bradford Bulls v Newcastle Knights, 1 February 2002

St John Ellis
keeps warm

Castleford v Leigh, 20 February 1994

A fan in Cardiff, 4 May 2008

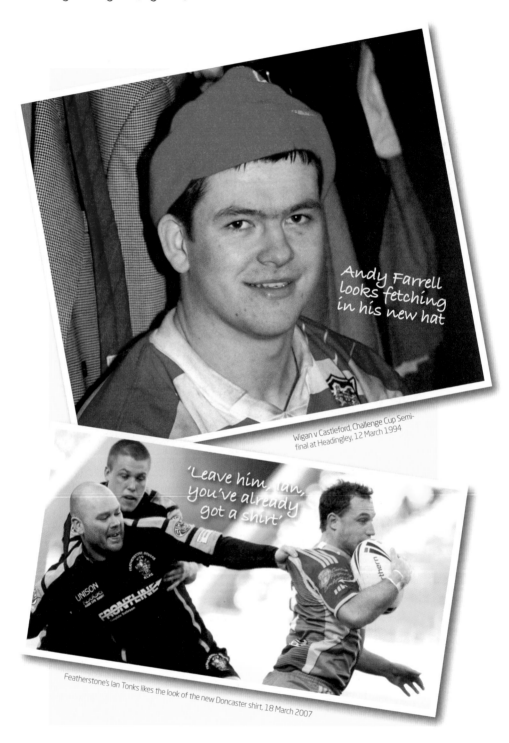

Andy Farrell
looks fetching
in his new hat

Wigan v Castleford, Challenge Cup Semi-
final at Headingley, 12 March 1994

'Leave him, Ian,
you've already
got a shirt'

Featherstone's Ian Tonks likes the look of the new Doncaster shirt, 18 March 2007

Stuart Fielden tries the latest body armour from Australia

9 August 2006

Byron Ford tries on a new hat

LHF Healthplan Division 1 Grand Final, 8 October 2006

'No, that's the other Michael Jackson and friend'

Wakefield's Michael Jackson at the 1991 Great Britain photo call, Wigan

'ET phone home!'

Tevita Leo-Latu models a new scrum cap, 5 September 2008

'I said put your shirt in the wash!'

Mark Jones, West Bowling v Leigh MR, 9 February 2008

One hell of a hang-over

Warrington fan, Cardiff, 6 May 2007

'Do I look good in these or what?'

David Wrench, 1 August 2004

A Salford fan after a night on the tiles

13 June 2004

Nathan Sykes gets help to fasten his scrum cap

9 June 2001

45

3

The Eyes Have it

From the moment a youngster first picks up a rugby ball, their coach will drill into them, 'Keep your eye on the ball'. But, while that's usually true, there are plenty of other things players have to focus on during a rugby league match. Our photographs find a few wandering eyes over the next chapter.

Blind-side prop?'

Michael Smith has view blocked by Jason Demetriou, Castleford Tigers v Wakefield Trinity Wildcats, Super League IX, 17 April 2004

The Normanton Knights help Nick Broere look for his contact lens, Normanton Knights v Edinburgh Eagles, Carnegie Challenge Cup 1st Round, 2 February 2008

Richard Baker celebrates a try, Doncaster v Villeneuve, Challenge Cup 5th Round, 24 February 2002

'My arm's gone blue!'

Dean Sampson, Castleford Tigers, Castleford v Odlham St Annes, Challenge Cup 4th Round, 13 February 2000

'Oh no—not Saints again'

Andy Farrell, Wigan Warriors

Dwain Chambers hypnotises the ball

31 March 2008

'I can't see a thing without my glasses'

Vince Fawcett tackles the goal post, Wigan Sevens, 5 August 1990

Martin Offiah realises he's scored at the wrong end

Wigan v Leeds in the Challenge Cup Final, 30th April 1994

Dave Clark (Barrow) looks for his contact lens

'There's something in my eye!'

Dave Lee, Sharlston Rovers v Oulton Raiders, National Cup 4th Round, 22 February 2003

'A, Z, M, W, P ...
I think ...'

Richard Chapman takes a pitch-side eye test, Featherstone Rovers v Villeneuve Leopards TXU Energi Challenge Cup
3rd Round, 26 January 2003

Gary Connolly checks the programme to see if he's playing

Great Britain photo call 1992

'How do you get a drink out of this cup?'

Leeds Rhinos 33 v St Helens 6, engage Super League XII Grand Final, Old Trafford, 13 October 2007

'I can't do this Rubik's Cube!'

Kevin Sinfield, Leeds Rhinos 11 v Melbourne Storm 4, Carnegie World Club Challenge, 29 February 2008

'Look into my eyes!'

Cyril Stacul tries to hypnotise the ball, Featherstone Rovers v Catalans Dragons, Carnegie Challenge Cup 4th Round, 20 April 2008

'Is that a goldfish?'

Alan Tait and Martin Offiah examine the Lancashire Cup. Widnes v Salford, Lancashire Cup Final, September 1990

'Where's the ball gone?'

Jon Wilkin, St Helens 28 v Hull FC 16, Carnegie Challenge Cup Final, Wembley, 30 August 2008

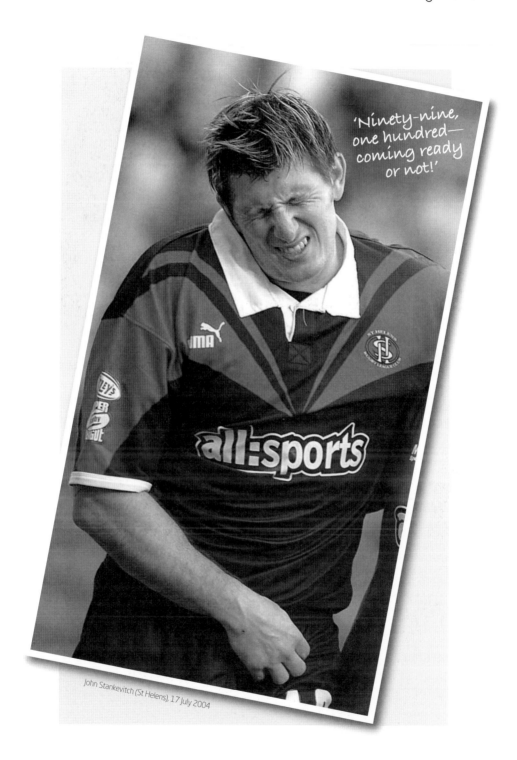

'Ninety-nine, one hundred— coming ready or not!'

John Stankevitch (St Helens), 17 July 2004

4

Hands, Knees and Other Body Parts

Rugby league might be primarily a handling sport, but just about every part of the body can be brought into play at different stages of the match. Aside from the obvious feet, shoulders and arms, players' noses, teeth and even some intimate regions can find themselves the focus of unwanted attention. And that's before we even mention a few head-turning hairstyles from recent years!

Damien Blanch can't get his boots off

Wakefield Trinity Wildcats 24 v Harlequins RL 20, Super League XIII Round 12, 26 April 2008

Bob Beswick double checks the instructions on the bottle of hair restorer

5 November 2008

Austin Buchanan gets a leg up from the opposition

24 February 2008

Danny Stocks and Shaun Flynn compare hair styles

Bramley Buffaloes v Hemel Stags, LHF Division 3 Final, 8 October 2006

'That tooth still hurts!'

Daniel Frame ponders, Dewsbury v Keighley, 23 July 2000

Body waxes can be painful

Gary Freeman receives treatment during the Great Britain v New Zealand 1st Test, Wembley, 16th October 1993

'Bendy Hendy'

Henderson Gill's wiggle was famous, Wigan v New Zealand, 1989

Paul Hicks has his nose picked

Dewsbury Rams v Gateshead Thunder, National League 2, 30 May 2004

Hitching a ride

Great Britain v New Zealand, 3rd Gillette Fusion Test at Wigan, 10th November 2007

Jonathan Griffiths chills out

Wigan 13 v St Helens 8, 1991 Challenge Cup Final, Wembley

Batley Tripod

Anthony Henderson finds it easier to balance on three legs, 22 February 2009

Andy Hobson

24 March 2002

Craig Huby has four arms and four legs

Castleford Tigers v Featherstone Rovers, pre-season friendly, 26 December 2007

How many fingers?

Search Plus

Dave Clark (Barrow Border Raiders) has his view blocked by Sean Richardson, Dewsbury v Barrow

Willie Talau tries some dentistry on Rod Jensen, Huddersfield v St Helens, 24 March 2008

Paul Johnson takes a bite out of Ryan Clayton, Castleford Tigers 31 v Warrington Wolves 34, Super League XIII, 24 March 2008

'I'm starving!'

Time for the turtles to take a rest

Leeds v Wakefield, 2 May 2003

A Leigh player feels the pain of defeat, Dewsbury v Leigh, NFP Grand Final, 29 July 2000

Hair-raising
stuff from
Misili Manu

Orford
Investments Ltd

mha

1 January 2006

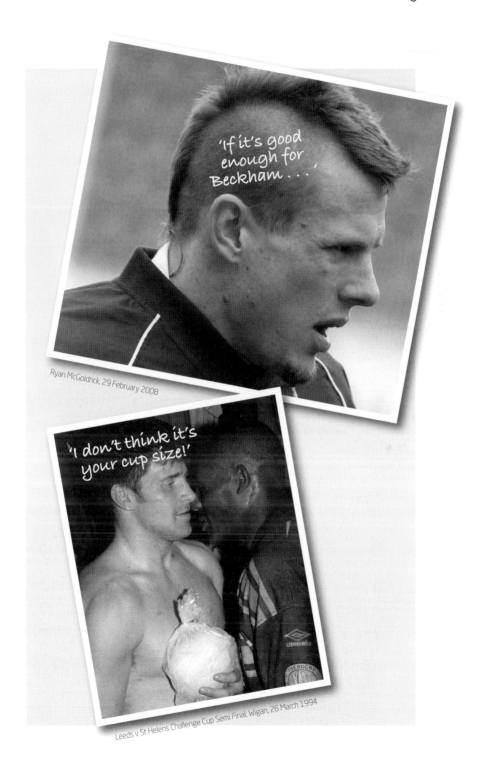

Ryan McGoldrick, 29 February 2008

'If it's good enough for Beckham . . .'

'I don't think it's your cup size!'

Leeds v St Helens Challenge Cup Semi Final, Wigan, 26 March 1994

'Can I have a gap in my teeth like that?'

Francis Meli points out Lee Briers' loose tooth, St Helens v Warrington 2007

'And you're playing at No. 6'

Australian captain, Mal Meninga, gives this Walters brother a haircut, World Cup photo call at Elland Road, 6 October 1992

A balancing act
by Richard Moore

Leeds v Wakefield, 26 December 2006

Dave Ingram, Dewsbury v Leigh, NFP Grand Final, 29 July 2000

Taking the medicine

'Nice Legs!'

Mark Mulligan, Bramley v Workington, 24 April 1994

Kevin Ward and Karl Fairbank on the subs bench at Wembley, First Test, Great Britain v Australia, 27 October 1990

Cool dude

Terry Newton, 11 May 2008

'It's my ball—you can't have it!'

Warrington v Catalans, 19 August 2007

'Keep still—it's all tangled'

Tawera Nikau finds that long hair can be a disadvantage, Castleford v Warrington, 24 September 1995

81

'Has your chewing gum lost its flavour?'

Roman Ovchinnikov, 16 March 2006

Adrian Morley feeling a bit horny

8 September 2005

James Roby wishes his arms were longer

Great Britain v New Zealand, 1st Gillette Fusion Test, 27 October 2007, Galpharm Stadium, Huddersfield

Gareth Raynor bares all in an interview

Hull FC 34 v St Helens 8, Powergen Challenge Cup Semi-final, 30 July 2005

Gary Sanderson is a hit with the girls!

Castleford v Warrington, 17 April 1994

85

Gary Schubert, Bramley v Workington Town, 24 April 1994

Quick—hide—the fuzz are coming!

Leeds Rhinos' Keith Senior and Jamie Jones-Buchanan, 7 September 2007

Chris Thorman removes an opponent's head

Huddersfield Giants v Widnes Vikings, Super League X, 11 March 2005

'Who stole my wig?'

Keith Senior in deep thought, 25 June 2004

The result of mating a rugby ball with a Bronco

Paul Sykes, Wakefield Trinity Wildcats v London Broncos, Super League VIII, 10 August 2003

This hearing aid isn't working very well

David Bradbury, Featherstone Rovers v Leigh Centurions, Powergen Challenge Cup 4th Round, 9 February 2003

A proud Jason Robinson in the Great Britain dressing room after the Test match

Great Britain v New Zealand, Wembley, 16 October 1993

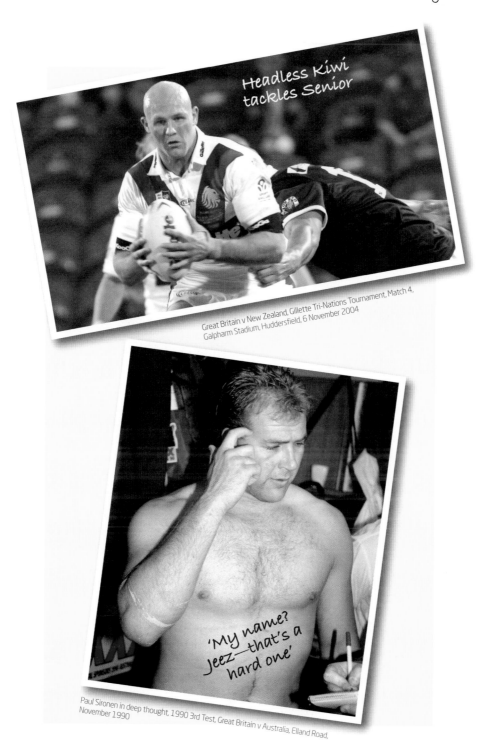

Headless Kiwi tackles Senior

Great Britain v New Zealand, Gillette Tri-Nations Tournament, Match 4,
Galpharm Stadium, Huddersfield, 6 November 2004

'My name? Jeez—that's a hard one'

Paul Sironen in deep thought, 1990 3rd Test, Great Britain v Australia, Elland Road,
November 1990

5

Float Like a Butterfly

Any Super League coach will tell you that agility is a key skill for any modern player to possess. Whether it's avoiding a covering defender or leaping to catch a pinpoint wide kick, rugby league players have to be exceptional on their feet. This can lead to some spectacular images, as we see over the next few pages.

It's Deon Bird's turn with the helium ball

29 February 2004

'I am not a parrot'

Brian Carney sits on a Kiwi's arm, Great Britain v New Zealand, Gillette
Tri-Nations Tournament, 4th Match, Galpharm Stadium, Huddersfield,
6 November 2004

Gavin Dodd kneels on the fence

Dewsbury v Widnes, 6 May 2008

Crouching
Giant—
Eastern
mysticism in
the Giants'
camp

Hefin O'Hare, 17 March 2002

'Gorilla in the Mist'

Ronnie 'Rambo' Gibbs dives over for a try, Wakefield v Castleford, 12 November 1989

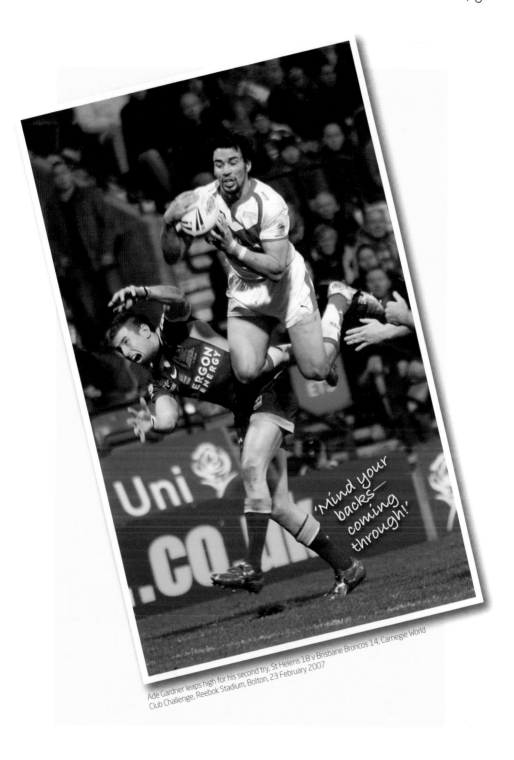

'Mind your backs— coming through!'

Ade Gardner leaps high for his second try, St Helens 18 v Brisbane Broncos 14, Carnegie World Club Challenge, Reebok Stadium, Bolton, 23 February 2007

Rob Jackson
tries one of the
new helium-
filled balls

Wakefield Trinity Wildcats v London Broncos, Super League VIII, 10 August 2003

'Hold still while I fasten your collar'

As a kid, Kris Radlinski thought he was an aeroplane, 31 August 2003

Mark Leafa is walking on air

Wakefield v Castleford, 21 March 2008

Getting the ball back off the roof

30 July 2005

Sam Obst looks on while Michael Korkidas floats away

Wakefield v Castleford, 21 March 2008

Gregory Mounis tries to float through the Leeds defence

Leeds v Catalans, 22 February 2008

Two Saints players try to stop Henry Paul from floating away

Wakefield v St Helens, 6 March 1994

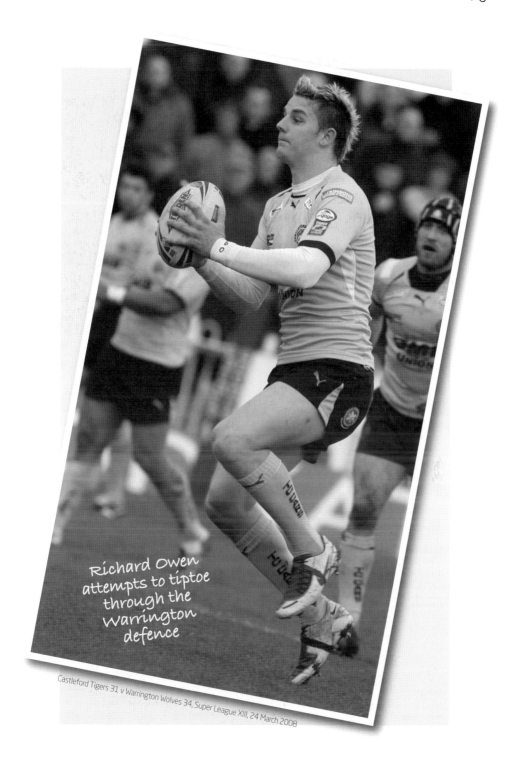

Richard Owen
attempts to tiptoe
through the
Warrington
defence

Castleford Tigers 31 v Warrington Wolves 34, Super League XIII, 24 March 2008

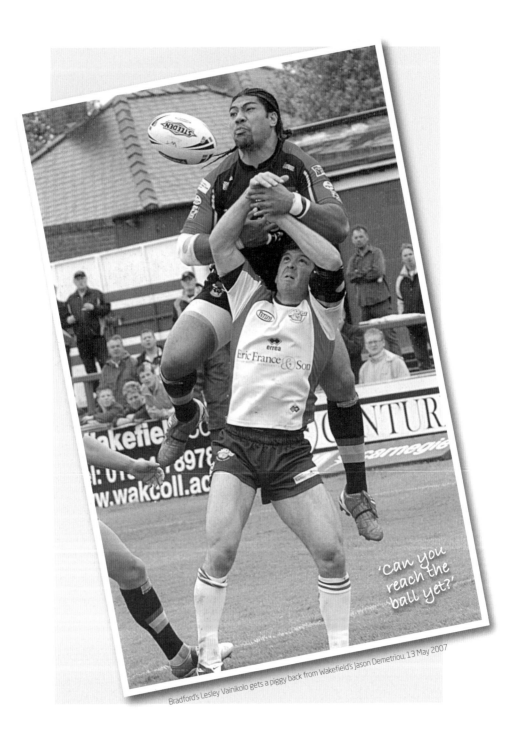

'can you reach the ball yet?'

Bradford's Lesley Vainikolo gets a piggy back from Wakefield's Jason Demetriou, 13 May 2007

Gravity doesn't work so well in Dewsbury

6 October 2008

6
Frightened of No-one

In a sport as physical as rugby league, there is simply no room for backing down to opponents on the field. As we see over the next few pages, there are more than a couple of ways to try and intimidate the opposition—and not all of them are limited to after the referee's whistle blows! Look out for a particularly brave Rob Burrow facing up to a host of fearsome New Zealanders.

The Samoan Haka

Samoa 38 v Lebanon 16, 2008 World Cup Qualifying Repechage Final, Chris Moyles Stadium, Featherstone, 14 November 2007

Lee Close comes face to face with Brendon Lindsay (6)

Dewsbury Rams v Sheffield Eagles, Carnegie Challenge Cup 4th Round, 1 April 2007

105

Widnes' Dean Gaskell considers his options during Dewsbury's 'Hug a Player' event

6 May 2008

Rob Burrow single-handedly faces up to the Kiwi Haka

Great Britain v New Zealand, 1st Gillette Fusion Test, Galpharm Stadium, Huddersfield, 27 October 2007

'It costs how much to get into a match?'

11 July 2004

Barrie
McDermott
'the enforcer'

Brad Fittler
has a rest

Great Britain v Australia, 2nd Test, 17 November 2001

'I can probably get through that gap'

Joe Mbu runs at Jamie Field, Wakefield Trinity Wildcats v
Harlequins RL, engage Super League XI Round 11,
23 April 2006

Scrum halves have to learn how to look mean

Stanningley v Glasson Rangers, 19 January 2008

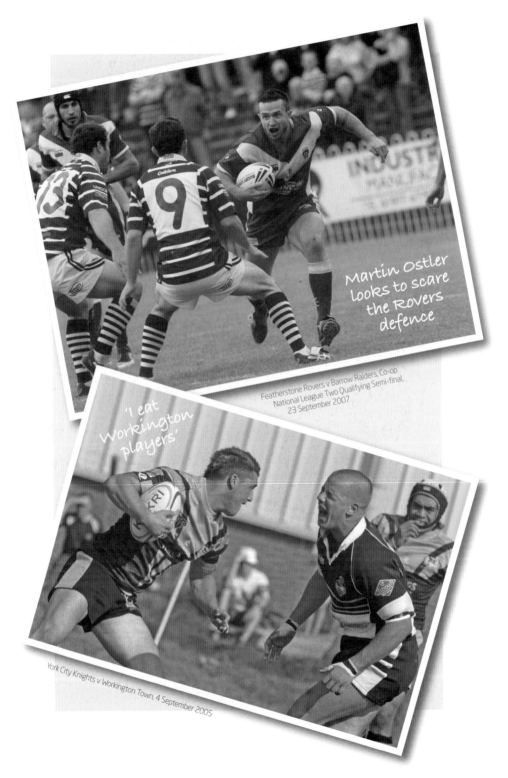

Martin Ostler
looks to scare
the Rovers
defence

Featherstone Rovers v Barrow Raiders, Co-op
National League Two Qualifying Semi-final,
23 September 2007

'I eat
Workington
players'

York City Knights v Workington Town, 4 September 2005

Rugby league is a sport for athletes

Aran Simm, Normanton Knights v Edinburgh Eagles, Carnegie Challenge Cup 1st Round, 2 February 2008

'You lookin' at me?'

Jon Scales (Halifax Blue Sox), Castleford, 19 August 2008

'Have they gone yet?'

Ricky Stuart, Wigan v Australia, 1990

11 July 2004

113

7
Shall we Dance?

Rugby league players can be an affectionate bunch, despite the brutal nature of the sport. Post-match group baths might be a thing of the past, but players can still get up close and personal in a few compromising situations—and not always intentionally!

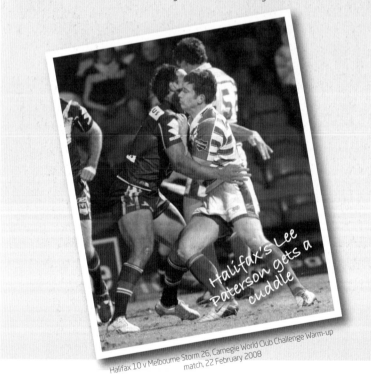

Halifax's Lee Paterson gets a cuddle

Halifax 10 v Melbourne Storm 26, Carnegie World Club Challenge Warm-up match, 22 February 2008

This Edinburgh Eagle knows all the latest dance moves

Normanton Knights v Edinburgh Eagles, Carnegie Challenge Cup 1st Round, 2 February 2008

'Never mind the ball—let's dance!'

Aerial ballet as the ball eludes Gary Connolly and Ellery Hanley.
Wigan 26 v Leeds 16, Challenge Cup Final, Wembley,
30 April 1994

French
dancing
lessons

Bradford v Catalans, 9 September 2007

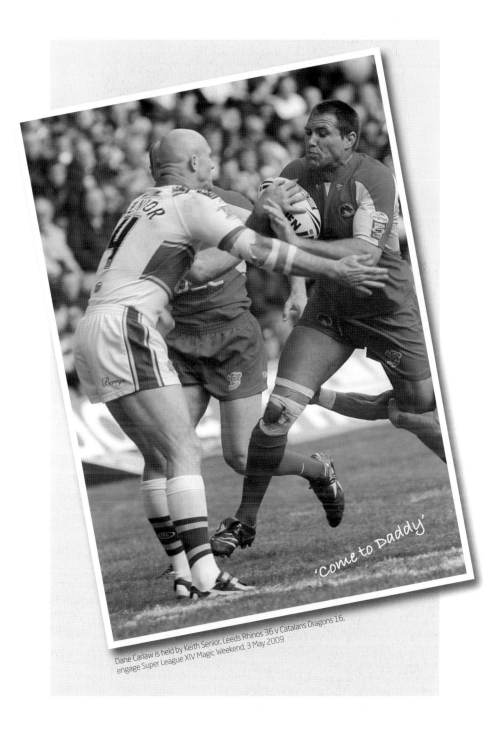

'Come to Daddy'

Dane Carlaw is held by Keith Senior, Leeds Rhinos 36 v Catalans Dragons 16,
engage Super League XIV Magic Weekend, 3 May 2009

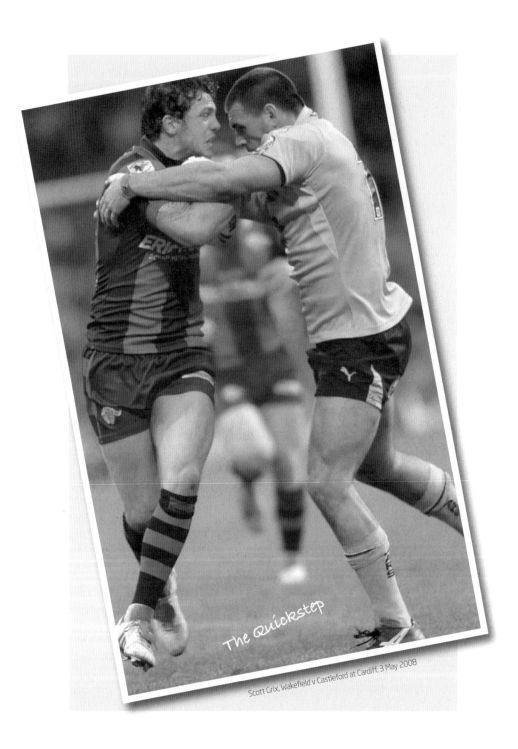

The Quickstep

Scott Grix, Wakefield v Castleford at Cardiff, 3 May 2008

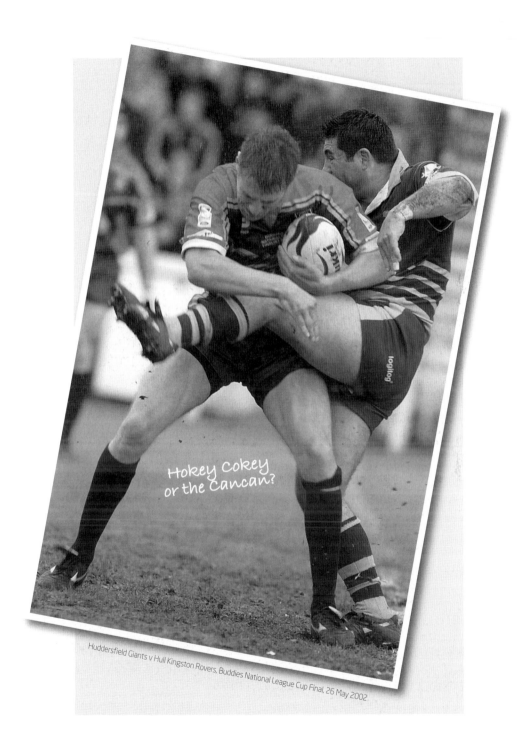

Hokey Cokey
or the Cancan?

Huddersfield Giants v Hull Kingston Rovers, Buddies National League Cup Final, 26 May 2002

119

'Give us a cuddle'

Graham Holroyd, Dewsbury Rams v Halifax, Co-op National League One, 5 August 2007

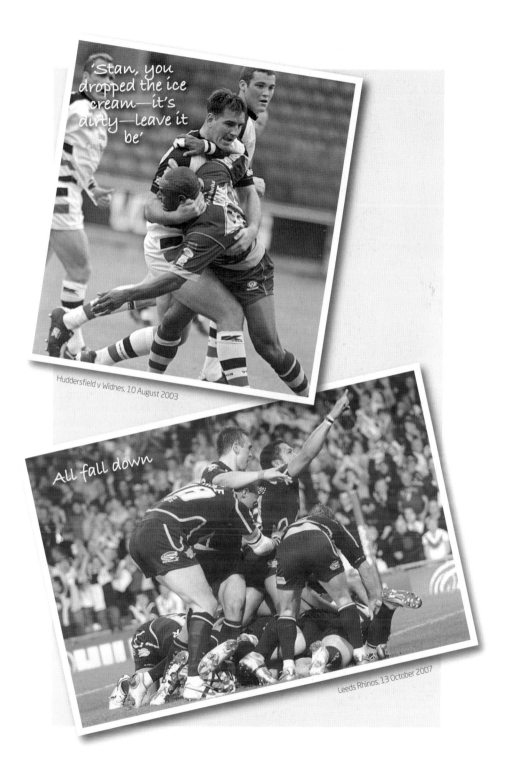

'Stan, you dropped the ice cream—it's dirty—leave it be'

Huddersfield v Widnes, 10 August 2003

All fall down

Leeds Rhinos, 13 October 2007

'It's my turn to lead'

Rob Burrow celebrates his try by dancing with Jamie Jones Buchanan, Great Britain v New Zealand, 3rd Gillette Fusion Test, Wigan, 10 November 2007

'Is it left leg first?'

Danny Tickle and Sione Faumuina, Castleford v Hull FC, 3 May 2009

John Stankevitch and Michael Korkidas doing a Quickstep Wakefield v Widnes. 15 May 2005

Paul Rauhihi and Sam Burgess, Bradford v Warrington, 16 March 2008

8
The Lighter Side

Super League might be big business now, but it's not always serious stuff in rugby league. Players from the 13-a-side code often have the ability to laugh at themselves—and looking at the pictures in this chapter it's just as well!

Leeds Rhinos take spelling lessons

FEILD ASSISTANT

2 February 2008

'Is this 10 metres ref?'

Bradford v Leeds, Challenge Cup Final, Murrayfield, 2000

'Two pints when you're ready'

Wakefield Trinity Wildcats v Warrington Wolves, Super League XIII Round 10,
6 April 2008

Superman Brent Webb flies with the birds

Leeds v Wigan, 31 May 2008

'The cross-bar isn't all that high!'

Rob Burrow surrenders, Leeds 11 v Melbourne Storm 4, Carnegie World Club Challenge, Elland Road, 29 February 2008

Catalans play against Les Invisibles

Bradford, 9 September 2007

'Spot the ball'

Sean Gleeson, Wakefield Trinity Wildcats v Warrington Wolves, Super League XIII Round 10, 6 April 2008

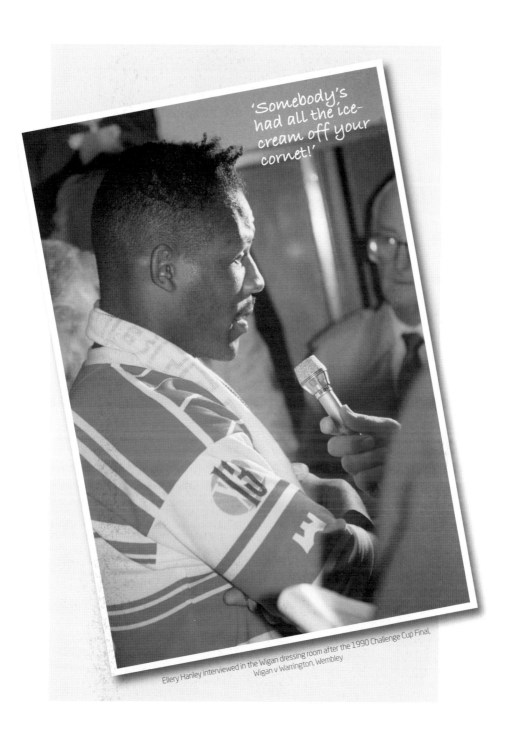

'Somebody's had all the ice-cream off your cornet!'

Ellery Hanley interviewed in the Wigan dressing room after the 1990 Challenge Cup Final, Wigan v Warrington, Wembley

Is Rob Burrow shrinking?

30 May 2002

'All in a neat line children!'

St Augustine's (St Helens) 20 v St Peter's (Wigan) 4, curtain raiser to Powergen Challenge Cup Final, Millennium Stadium, Cardiff, 26 April 2003

Wakefield's Richard Moore tries out the new invisible rugby ball

Wakefield v Castleford at Cardiff, 3 May 2008

'How do I get my finger out of here?'

Wigan v Leeds, Premiership Final, 21 May 1999, Old Trafford

'I told you not to ring me at work'

Martin Gleeson, England v Wales, Gillette Fusion International, Keepmoat Stadium, Doncaster, 10 October 2008

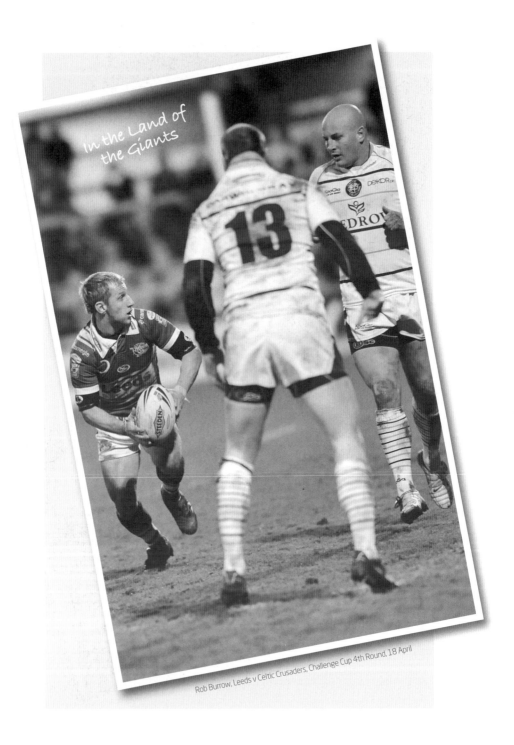

In the Land of the Giants

Rob Burrow, Leeds v Celtic Crusaders, Challenge Cup 4th Round, 18 April

'He went that way'

Danny Grimshaw makes a break, Sharlston Rovers v Drighlington, Halbro Yorkshire Cup Semi-final, 17 November 2007

'The coach said pass it to number 9'

Les Holliday faces a dilemma playing for Widnes v Bradford, 1990 Premiership Final, Old Trafford (the two numbers 9s are Phil McKenzie (left) and Brian Noble)

Simon Mannering looks for a gap whilst his team mates surrender

Great Britain v New Zealand, 3rd Gillette Fusion Test at Wigan, 10 November 2007

Champion

Ali Lauitiiti is very relaxed

Leeds Rhinos v St Helens, engage Super League Grand Final at Old Trafford, 4 October 2008

'Hands up – who wants to see that again?'

Martin Offiah takes a closer look at the crowd,
Leeds v Widnes Premiership Semi-final match,
6 May 1990

Richard Owen surrenders

Castleford Tigers 31 v Warrington Wolves 34, Super League XIII, 24 March 2008

Wigan's secret weapon?

Henry Paul shows off the Rugby League Challenge Cup after Wigan beat Leeds, Challenge Cup Final, Wembley, 29 April 1995

'Just a bit to
the right'

Ray Price takes up his famous stance at Wakefield as Castleford take a kick at goal, 12 November 1989

'Spare a few pennies guv'ner?'

Wendell Sailor doesn't give a XXXX about the Leeds weather at the beginning of the 1994 Australian tour

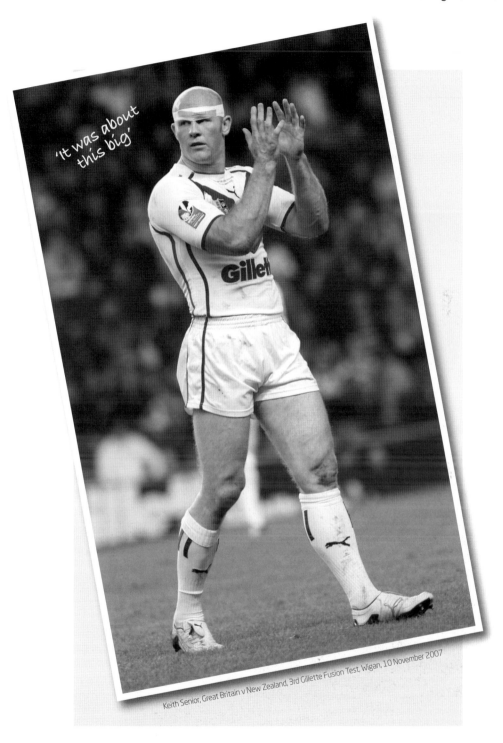

'It was about this big'

Keith Senior, Great Britain v New Zealand, 3rd Gillette Fusion Test, Wigan, 10 November 2007

'Just replacing some body fluids'

Kelvin Skerrett, Wigan 30 v Leeds 10, Challenge Cup Final at Wembley, 29 April 1995

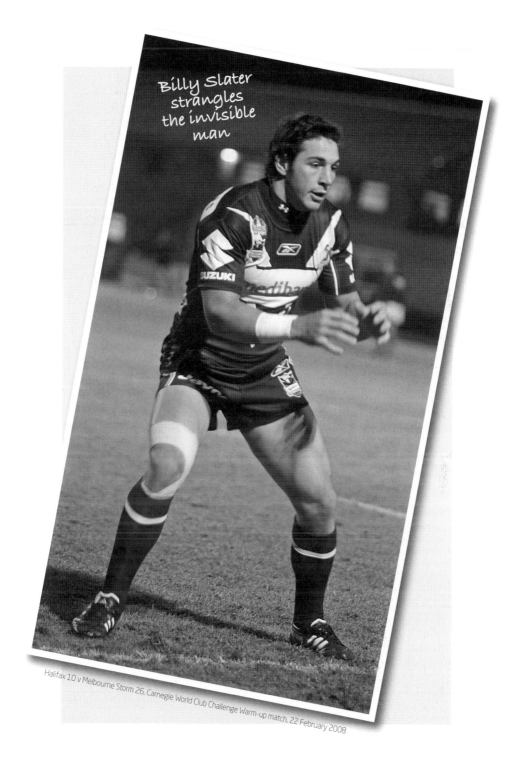

Billy Slater strangles the invisible man

Halifax 10 v Melbourne Storm 26, Carnegie World Club Challenge Warm-up match, 22 February 2008

Blowin' in
the wind

Danny Tickle lines up a conversion, Hull FC 24 v Castleford Tigers 16,
engage Super League XIV Magic Weekend, 3 May 2009

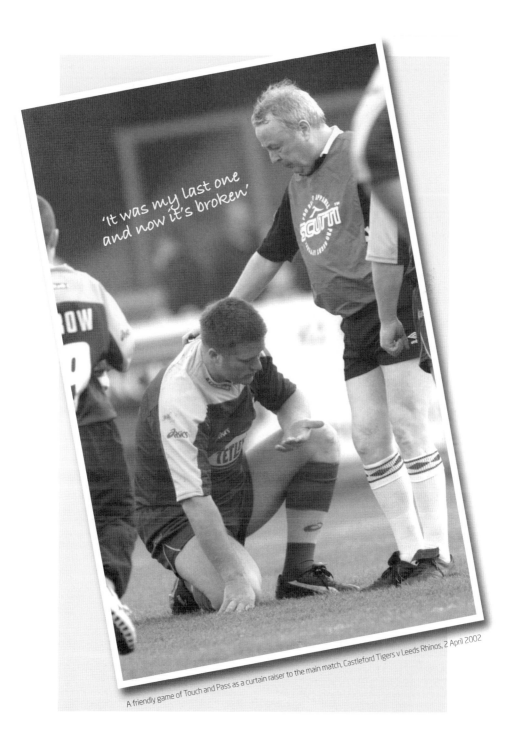

'It was my last one and now it's broken'

A friendly game of Touch and Pass as a curtain raiser to the main match, Castleford Tigers v Leeds Rhinos, 2 April 2002

145

'Where's the ball?'

Sean Richardson looks up Jamie Smith's sleeve for the ball, Dewsbury v Barrow Border Raiders

Two-man scrum

Rob Burrow and Jason Cayless, Leeds Rhinos 33 v St Helens 6, engage Super League XII Grand Final, Old Trafford, 13 October 2007

Martin Offiah looks surprised as he holds the Challenge Cup after Wigan beat Leeds, Challenge Cup Final, Wembley, 30 April 1994

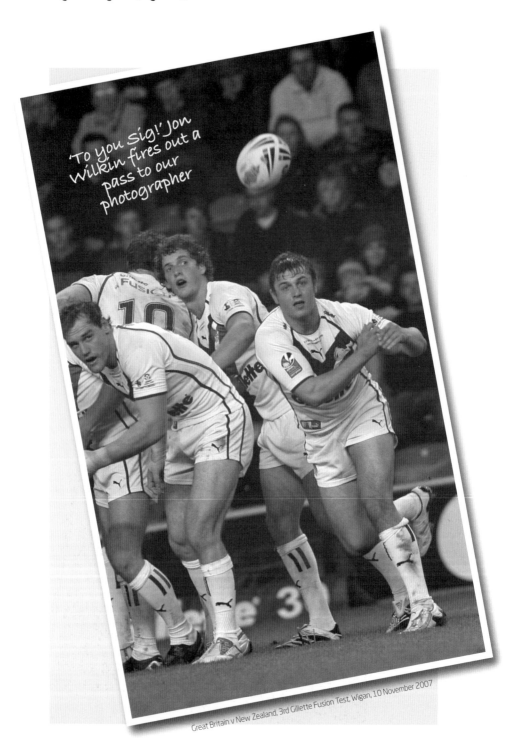

'To you Sig!' Jon Wilkin fires out a pass to our photographer

Great Britain v New Zealand, 3rd Gillette Fusion Test, Wigan, 10 November 2007

9
The Sweet Smell of Success

As we've already seen, rugby league can throw up plenty of memorable images from events on the field, but with 34 grown men taking each other on in every match, there's bound to be a few strange smells out on the field every now and then as well. As you can see from the pictures in this chapter, the sport isn't always a bed of roses for players' nostrils.

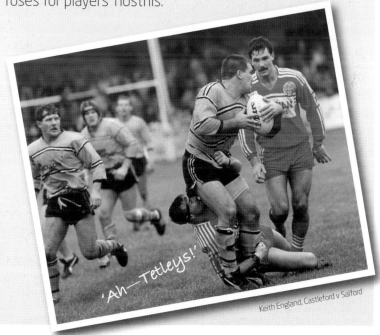

'Ah—Tetleys!'

Keith England, Castleford v Salford

Matt Geyer reacts to the Elland Road drains problem

Leeds Rhinos 11 v Melbourne Storm 4, Carnegie World Club Challenge, 29 February 2008

'Phew—it is me!'

Graham Mackay checks his deodorant with
Chris Smith, Castleford v Hull,
28 June 2002

Armpit
smelling
contest

Doncaster Dragons v Huddersfield Giants, Buddies National League Cup Semi-final, 19 May 2002

Andy Gregory says a prayer

Wigan v Warrington Challenge Cup
2nd Round tie, 16 February 1992

'I get so peckish during the match'

Jamie Thackray, Hull v Widnes, 10 April 2005

Sent off for having BO or for pretending to be Bobbie Goulding?

BY GOULDING

Tawera Nikau in the Headingley dressing room after the Rugby League Challenge Cup Semi-final, Castleford v Hull, 14 March 1992

Andy Hobson thinks about sitting down

Halifax v Wigan, 24 March 2002

Inga Tuigamala gets some accusing looks when a strange smell fills the Wigan dugout

Castleford v Wigan, RLCC Semi-final, Headingley, 12 March 1994

'The drains are up again!'

John Kear and Stuart Raper have a discussion about the drains at the JJB Stadium, Wigan v Hull, Kelloggs Nutri-Grain Challenge Cup 4th Round, 9 February 2002

'Don't sit!'

St Helens' Apollo Perelini hopes that Adrian Vowles keeps his balance

They won't go near Keiron Cunningham until he changes his deodorant

Leeds Rhinos 33 v St Helens 6, engage Super League XII Grand Final, Old Trafford, 13 October 2007

156

10
The Cheek of It!

With hundreds of collisions between players in every single game of rugby league, it's inevitable that some are going to find themselves in some uncompromising positions. When you're being dumped to the ground by two 17 stone bruisers, you don't have time to check if your shorts are properly covering your behind, or if your head or hands are in an unfortunate position. Look out for some cheeky images over the next few pages.

'No tongues!'

Sam Burgess and Brett Ferres get close, Bradford v Wakefield, 20 July 2008

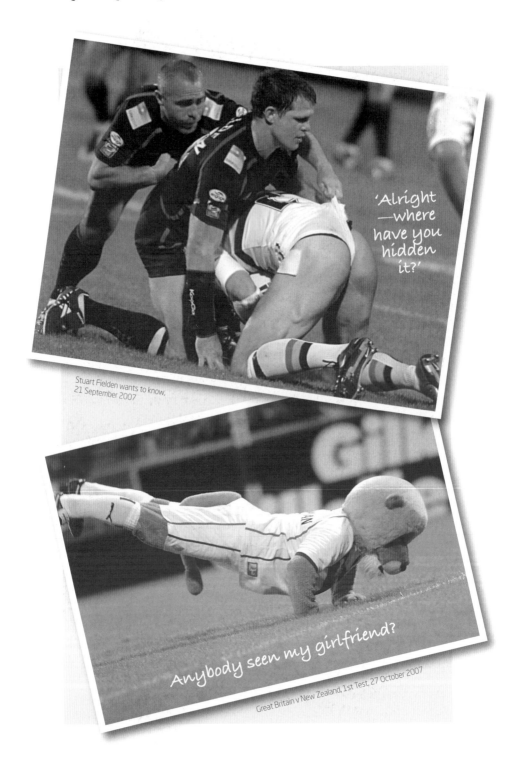

'Alright —where have you hidden it?'

Stuart Fielden wants to know,
21 September 2007

Anybody seen my girlfriend?

Great Britain v New Zealand, 1st Test, 27 October 2007

Two Dewsbury
tacklers make a wish

24 February 2008

Rob Burrow
keeps an eye on
Chris Thorman

Leeds Rhinos v London Broncos, Powergen Challenge
Cup 5th Round, 1 March 2003

'I think we've
been spotted'

Gareth Hock receives treatment from Mike Forshaw during the match, Wigan Warriors 38 v St Helens 18, engage Super League
XIV Magic Weekend, 2 May 2009

'Ten out of ten for cheek!'

Barrie McDermott, Great Britain 20 v Australia 12, 1st Test, McAlpine Stadium, Huddersfield, 11 November 2001

'Let me rub it better'

Michael Withers receives attention, Bradford Bulls v Leeds Rhinos, Super League IX Grand Final at Old Trafford, 16 October 2004

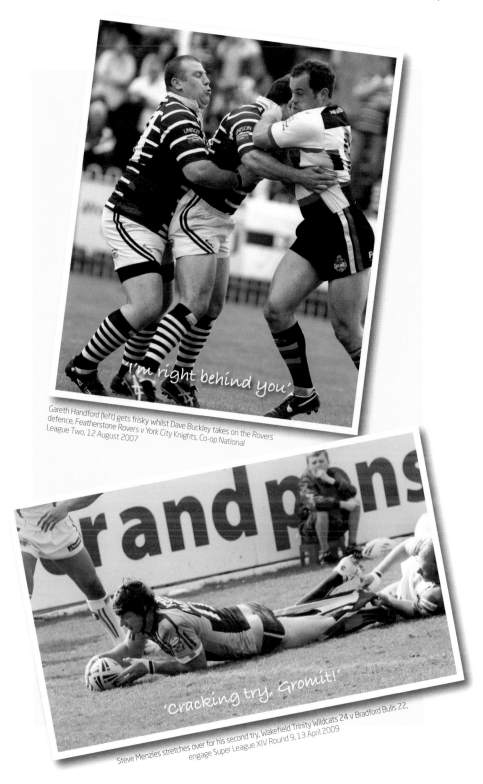

'I'm right behind you'

Gareth Handford (left) gets frisky whilst Dave Buckley takes on the Rovers defence, Featherstone Rovers v York City Knights, Co-op National League Two, 12 August 2007

'Cracking try, Gromit!'

Steve Menzies stretches over for his second try, Wakefield Trinity Wildcats 24 v Bradford Bulls 22, engage Super League XIV Round 9, 13 April 2009

Andy Coley
wants Craig
Huby to
check his
flies

Castleford Tigers v Wigan Warriors, Super League XIII Round 18, 22 June 2008

'Don't cry lad'

Simon Finnigan (Widnes) comforts Paul Smith, Huddersfield Giants v Widnes Vikings, Super League X, 11 March 2005

Paul Hulme makes sure Mike O'Neill in the Widnes defence is quick off the mark

Widnes v St Helens, RLCC Semi-final 1989

'Maoris are this big!'

Great Britain v New Zealand, Gillette Tri-Nations Game 6, KC Stadium, Hull, 20 November 2004

Clint
Newton
gets a
spanking

2 February 2008

Scott Murrell is toying with an idea

17 August 2007

Siddal v Queens, 11 April 2009

Shirts v
Skins

Stuart Cummings referees the
2000 World Cup Final

Kevin Ward
shows his legs
with Graham
Southernwood
as hooker

Castleford v Wigan, 1989

'No hard feelings?'

Steve Turner gets a kiss from Jon Goddard (3), Halifax 10 v Melbourne Storm 26, Carnegie World Club Challenge Warm-up match, 22 February 2008

'Let me tell you about the time...'

Ryan Hudson whispers in Willie Talau's ear, Huddersfield v St Helens, 24 March 2008

11
Un-officially

In such a high-octane, physical sport like rugby league, you need a man in the middle to keep a lid on matters. Referees can often find themselves the focus of attention on the pitch, and they are always immersed in the action from start to finish. And while the 'merry whistleblowers', as one television pundit likes to call them, might often be the subject of frustration from the terraces, without them there is no game. Here we see the lighter side of being a match official.

'Anybody seen my contact lens?'

Referee Phil Bentham, Salford v Bradford, 22 May 2009

'Don't hit me Stuart!'

Richard Silverwood defends himself,
Leeds v Wigan, 31 May 2008

'Behind you!'

Steve Ganson moves out of Sean Long's way, Wigan Warriors 38 v St Helens 18, engage Super League XIV Magic
Weekend, 2 May 2009

'What do you do with a touch judge's flag?'

Steve Campbell, Sharlston Rovers v Glasson Rangers, BARLA National Cup 1st Round, 11 December 2004

'Paul, they were this big!'

Ronnie Laughton explains to Paul Deacon,
Castleford v Bradford, 18 May 2008

'Robbie Paul—this is your life!'

Harry Gration carries the famous red book, Powergen Challenge Cup Final, 26 April 2003, Millennium Stadium, Cardiff

'You watch my back,
and I'll watch yours'

Steve Ganson makes sure all the officials are
plugged in, Castleford Tigers 31 v Warrington
Wolves 34, Super League XIII,
24 March 2008

'Nice boots!'

Steve Nicholson (referee), Featherstone Rovers v Leigh Centurions, 16 June 2002

177

'And here is your change!'

French referee Alain Sablayrolles tries to explain to Ellery Hanley and Mal Meninga, 2nd Test at Old Trafford, 10 November 1990

Lesley Vainikolo tries to out-stare Ian Smith

Bradford v Catalans, 25 March 2007

Ashley Klein shows Lee Briers who's boss

Bradford Bulls v Warrington Wolves, engage Super League XII Round 12, 29 April 2007

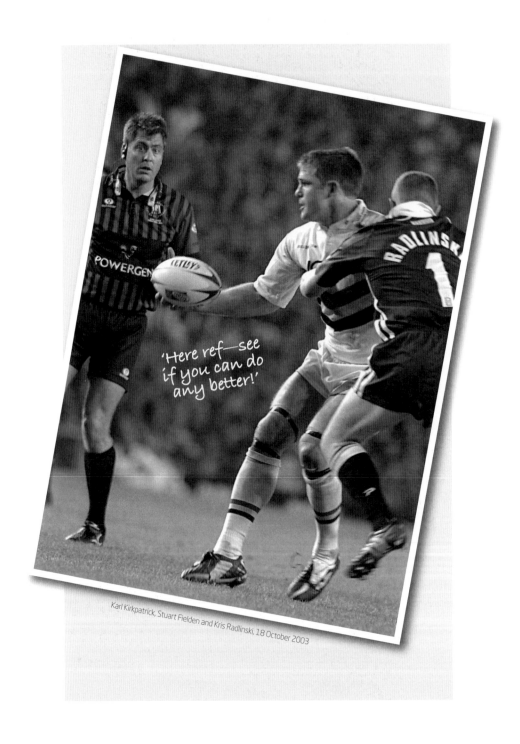

Karl Kirkpatrick, Stuart Fielden and Kris Radlinski, 18 October 2003

Steve Ganson shows Sean Penkywicz which end is which,
Halifax 10 v Melbourne Storm 26, Carnegie
World Club Challenge Warm-up match,
22 February 2008

Castleford v Leigh, 20 February 1994

'Ref, you really ought to move!'

David Hodgson and Phil Bentham (referee), Castleford Tigers v Salford City Reds, Engage Super League XI Round 12, 30 April 2006

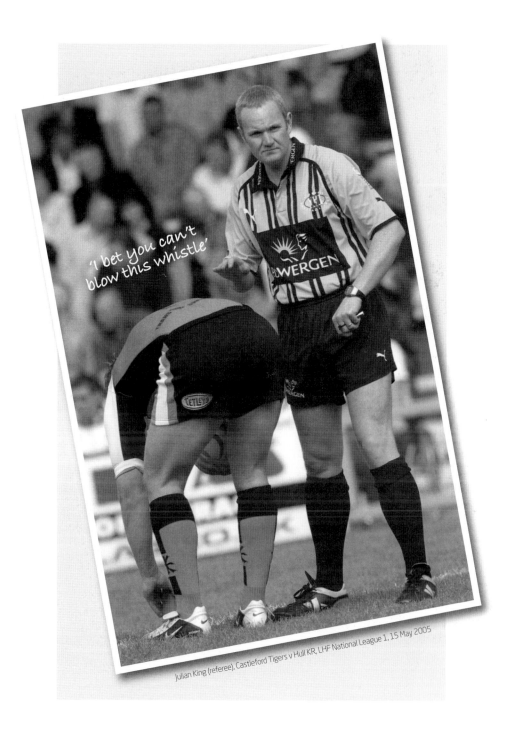

'I bet you can't blow this whistle'

Julian King (referee), Castleford Tigers v Hull KR, LHF National League 1, 15 May 2005

'I'll escort you to the touchline if you promise not to come back for 10 minutes'

Bradford Bulls v Warrington Wolves, engage Super League XII Round 12, 29 April 2007

'Nice arse, but you need to shed a couple of pounds'

Steve Presley, Sharlston Rovers v Huddersfield Sharks, GMB Cup, 22 January 2005

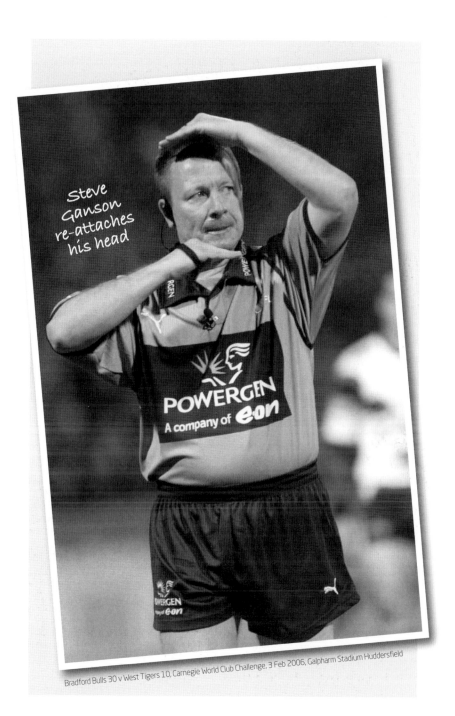

Steve
Ganson
re-attaches
his head

Bradford Bulls 30 v West Tigers 10, Carnegie World Club Challenge, 3 Feb 2006, Galpharm Stadium Huddersfield

Steve Ganson misplaces his whistle

Castleford Tigers 31 v Warrington Wolves 34, Super League XIII, 24 March 2008

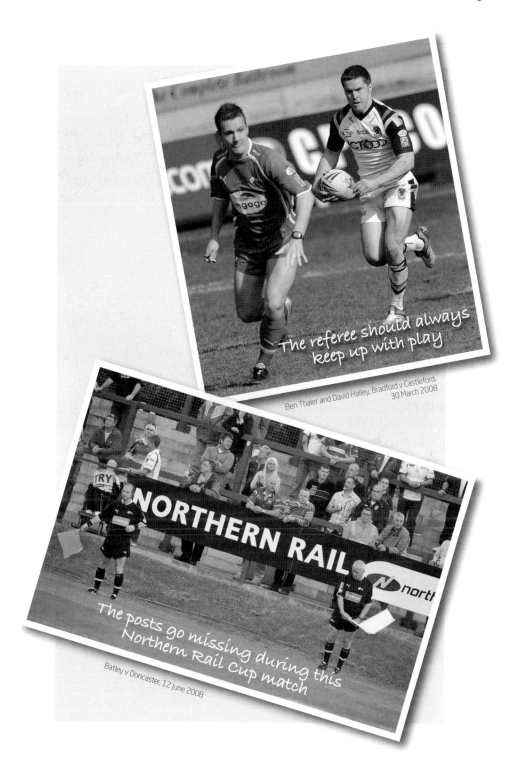

The referee should always keep up with play

Ben Thaler and David Halley, Bradford v Castleford, 30 March 2008

The posts go missing during this Northern Rail Cup match

Batley v Doncaster, 12 June 2008

'Too much facial hair Keiron'

Ashley Klein explains to Keiron Cunningham, Leeds Rhinos 33 v St Helens 6, engage Super League XII Grand Final, Old Trafford, 13 October 2007

'What sort of a Pom?'

Mal Meninga gets a lecture from Ray Tennant, Leeds v Australia tour match, 21 October 1990

Paul Wellens looks to see if Steve Ganson is up with play, St Helens 28 v Hull FC 16, Carnegie Challenge Cup Final, Wembley, 30 August 2008

12

Ouch!

Rugby league is a tough, uncompromising sport—the toughest in the world if you listen to those who have played the game. And while that makes for an exciting, brutal spectacle, it inevitably leads to injuries on a regular basis. Injuries are part and parcel of playing rugby league, and the high impact nature of the sport results in some spectacular photographs. The images in this chapter paint a graphic picture of how much players put their bodies on the line every week. Perhaps Graham Lowe, the former Wigan coach, put it as well as anyone. 'I'm 49, I've had a brain haemorrhage and a triple bypass and I could still go out and play a reasonable game of rugby union,' Lowe said, 'but I wouldn't last 30 seconds in rugby league.'

Kevin Beardmore is carried off

Castleford v Bradford Yorkshire Cup Final, Headingley, 17 October 1987

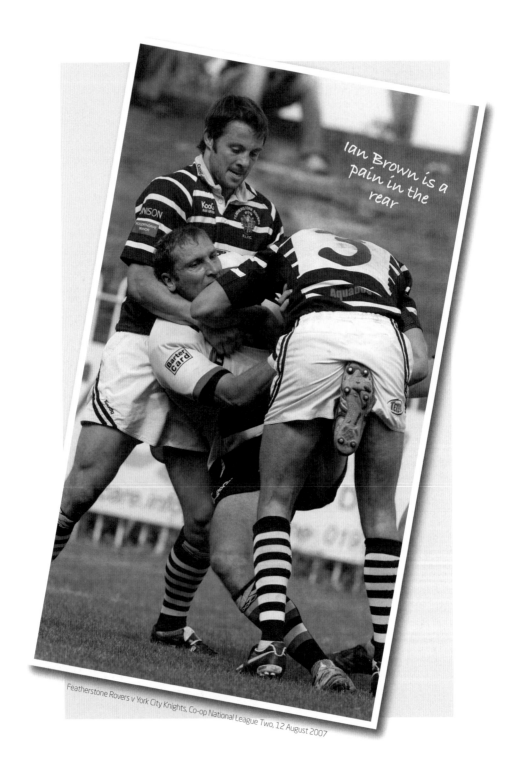

Ian Brown is a pain in the rear

Featherstone Rovers v York City Knights, Co-op National League Two, 12 August 2007

'Ouch!' Craig Calvert gets one for his trouble

Halifax v Whitehaven match, 23 September 2007

Danny Brough receives attention

Wakefield v Huddersfield, 15 June 2008

Dane Carlaw receives attention

Warrington v Catalans, 21 February 2009

Remi Casty needs help with his yoga position

21 February 2009

Lee Gilmour battles on in pain

4 February 2007

'Come on—you're playing scrum-half!'

Stuart Dickens drags his new team mate kicking and screaming on to the pitch, Featherstone v Salford, 22 May 2008

Kirk Yeaman feels the pain

Catalans v Hull FC, 21 June 2007

Paul Deacon is stretchered off

Bradford v Wakefield, 9 March 2003

Two Dewsbury tacklers try to save their Widnes colleague from disappearing down a rabbit hole

Dewsbury v Widnes, 6 May 2008

David Ferriol shows that rugby league is indeed a contact sport

9 September 2007

Brent Tate is led from the field

World Cup group match, Australia v New Zealand, 26 October 2008

'On my head, son!'

Hull KR's Kris Welham is tackled, Warrington Wolves 28 v Hull KR 36, engage Super League XIV Magic Weekend, 3 May 2009

Shontayne Hape is 'tackled' by Danny McGuire

Great Britain v New Zealand, Gillette Tri-Nations Tournament, Match 4, Galpharm Stadium, Huddersfield, 6 November 2004

'He's not very bendy!'

Wakefield's Nathan Wood gets to grips with Halifax's Andrew Dunemann, Halifax v Wakefield, 10 March 2002

Bradford's Lesley Vainikolo feels the weight of the Salford defence, 24 February 2006

'It was him!'

Richard Horne, 30 January 2002

Face painting gone wrong

Gary Hulse (Widnes), 6 March 2005

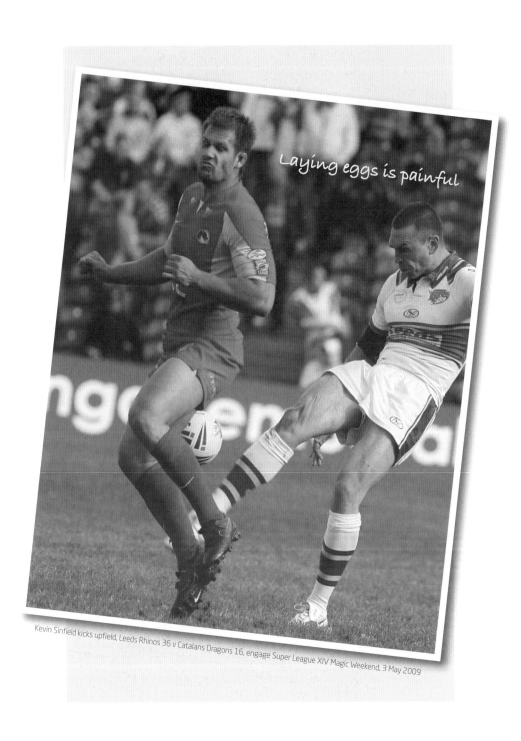

Laying eggs is painful

Kevin Sinfield kicks upfield, Leeds Rhinos 36 v Catalans Dragons 16, engage Super League XIV Magic Weekend, 3 May 2009

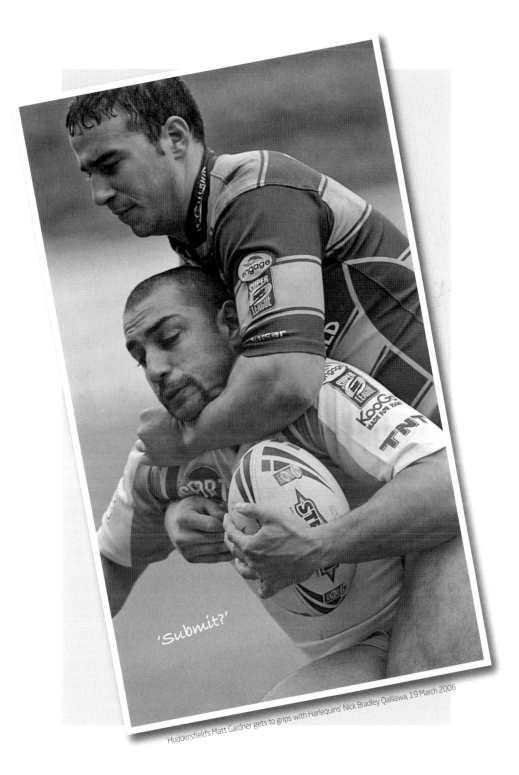

'Submit?'

Huddersfield's Matt Gardner gets to grips with Harlequins' Nick Bradley Qalilawa, 19 March 2006

Jessie Joe Parker receives treatment, PNG v England World Cup group match, 25 October 2008

Nick Fozzard
is collared

Bradford Bulls v Hull KR, 15 February 2009

13

But Seriously

'The day that God invented rugby league he didn't do anything else but sit around and feel good.' Those were the words of legendary Australian coach Jack Gibson, and it's a sentiment echoed by people involved in a sport that is often labelled 'The Greatest Game'.

Passion, comradeship, breath-taking skill and excitement are just some of the qualities that make rugby league so special —qualities that a camera lens can capture perfectly. Here we present just a small selection of our favourite images from 21 years covering this magical sport.

A very young Andy Farrell lifts the trophy after Wigan Under-15s won the curtain raiser to the 1989 Lancashire Cup Final

Dean Bell looks to offload to Joe Lydon

Wigan v St Helens, 1989 Challenge Cup Final, Wembley

The unmistakable shape of Frano Botica lining up yet another kick at goal, Wigan v Oldham, 1991 Rugby League Challenge Cup Semi-final, 23 March 1991

Leeds v New Zealand, 24 October 1993

Ellery Hanley on the way to a try

Wigan v Halifax, 1989 Regal Trophy final, Headingley

Sean Long dives in for his try

Hull KR 0 v St Helens 50, Powergen Challenge Cup Semi-final, 29 July 2006

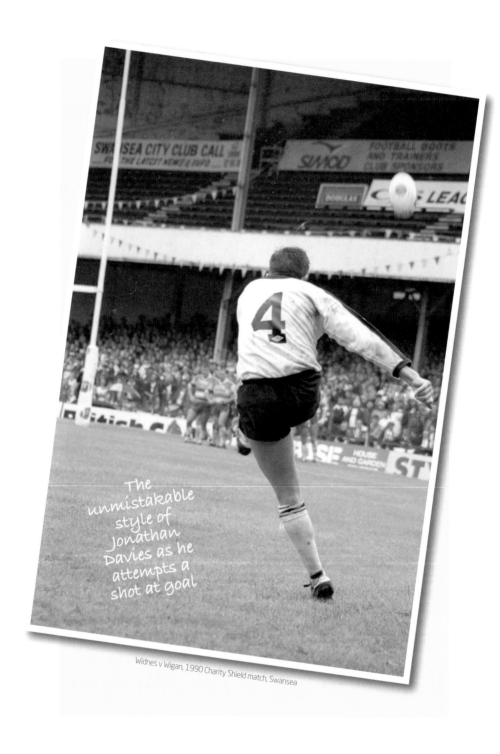

The unmistakable style of Jonathan Davies as he attempts a shot at goal

Widnes v Wigan, 1990 Charity Shield match, Swansea

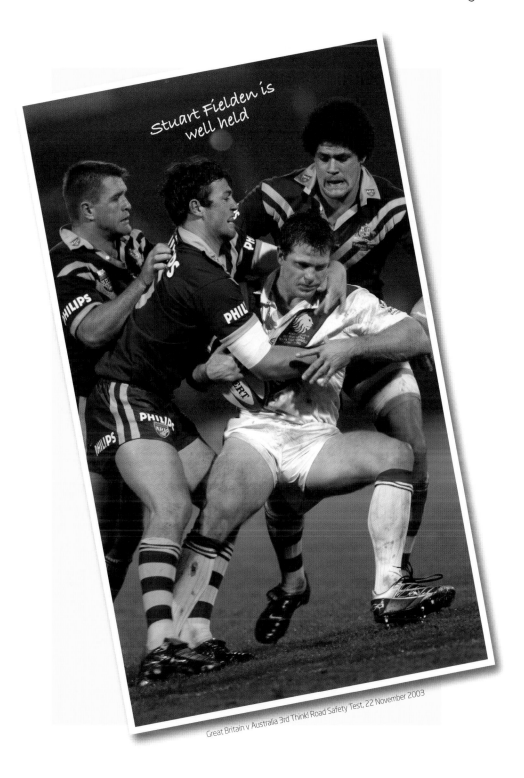

Stuart Fielden is well held

Great Britain v Australia 3rd Think! Road Safety Test, 22 November 2003

A youthful Sean Long in action

Lancashire Academy v Yorkshire, Featherstone, 9 May 1994

Lee Briers offloads

Huddersfield Giants v Warrington Wolves, 3 May 2008

Keiron Cunningham gets the ball to Paul Newlove for St Helens

St Helens v Wigan, 1997 Premiership Final, Old Trafford, 28 September 1997

215

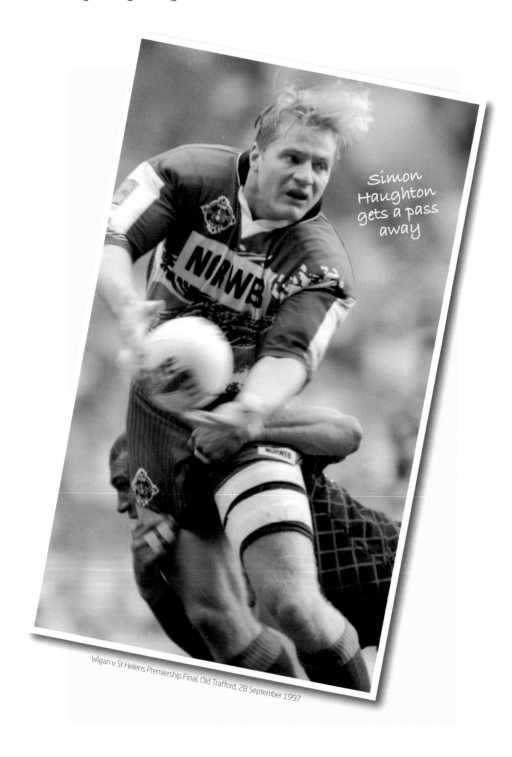

Simon Haughton gets a pass away

Wigan v St Helens Premiership Final, Old Trafford, 28 September 1997

Ellery Hanley in action for Wigan

Wakefield v Wigan, RLCC 3rd Round 1989/90 season

Gary Connolly chips ahead with Jason Robinson in support,
Great Britain v New Zealand 1st Test, Wembley, 16 October 1993

Lee Crooks

Castleford v Wigan, Regal Trophy Final, Headingley, 22 January 1994

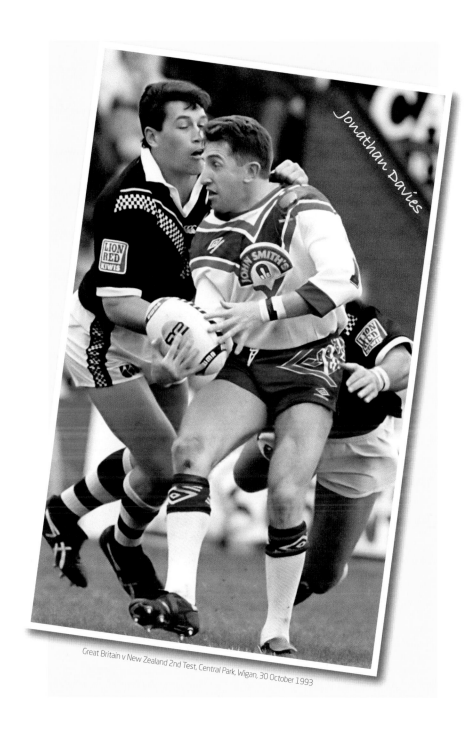

Jonathan Davies

Great Britain v New Zealand 2nd Test, Central Park, Wigan, 30 October 1993

Shaun Edwards takes to the air

Wigan 20 v Widnes 14, Rugby League Challenge Cup Final, 1993

Mike Gregory

Warrington v Oldham, Lancashire Cup Final, St Helens, 1989

Ellery Hanley skips past Paul Sironen at Old Trafford

Great Britain v Australia, 2nd Test, 10 November 1990

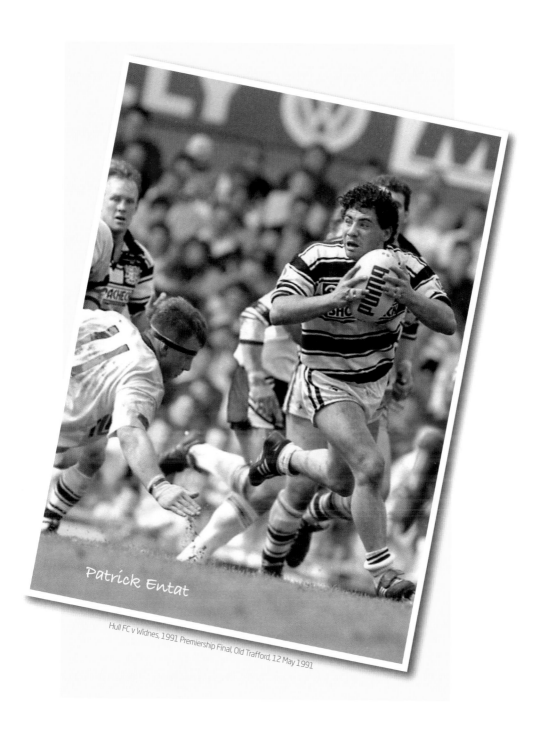

Patrick Entat

Hull FC v Widnes, 1991 Premiership Final, Old Trafford, 12 May 1991

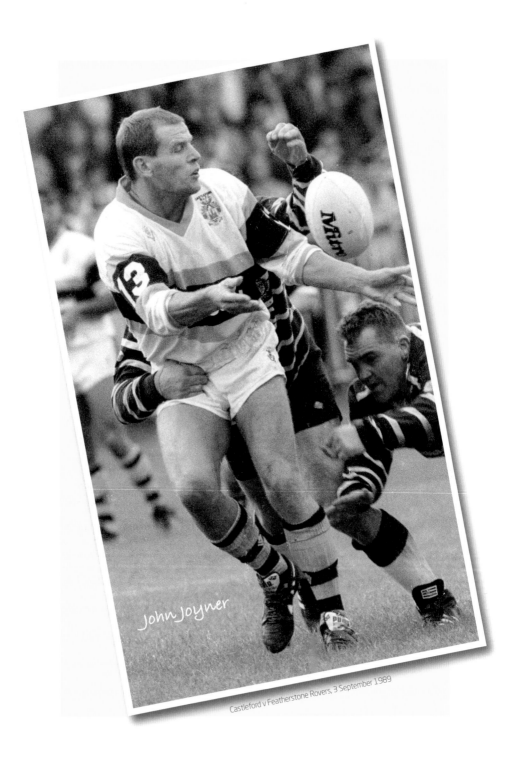

John Joyner

Castleford v Featherstone Rovers, 3 September 1989

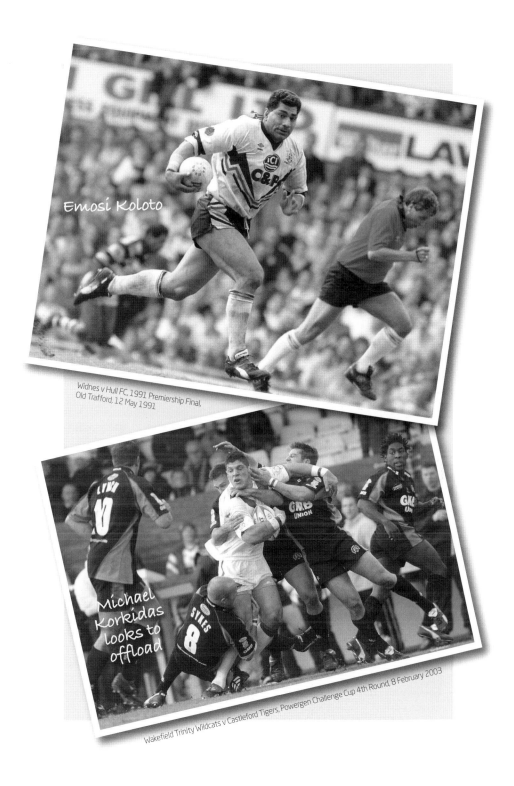

Emosi Koloto

Widnes v Hull FC, 1991 Premiership Final,
Old Trafford, 12 May 1991

Michael
Korkidas
looks to
offload

Wakefield Trinity Wildcats v Castleford Tigers, Powergen Challenge Cup 4th Round, 8 February 2003

Danny McGuire

Great Britain v New Zealand, 2nd Gillette Fusion Test,
KC Stadium, Hull, 3 November 2007

James Lowes dives over for a try despite the
attentions of Shaun Edwards and Kelvin Skerrett

Wigan 30 v Leeds 10, 1995 Rugby League Challenge Cup Final, 29 April 1995

Jon Whittle

Featherstone v Oldham, Divisional Play-offs, 7 October 2007

Kevin Ward

Castleford v Hull, 5 March 1989

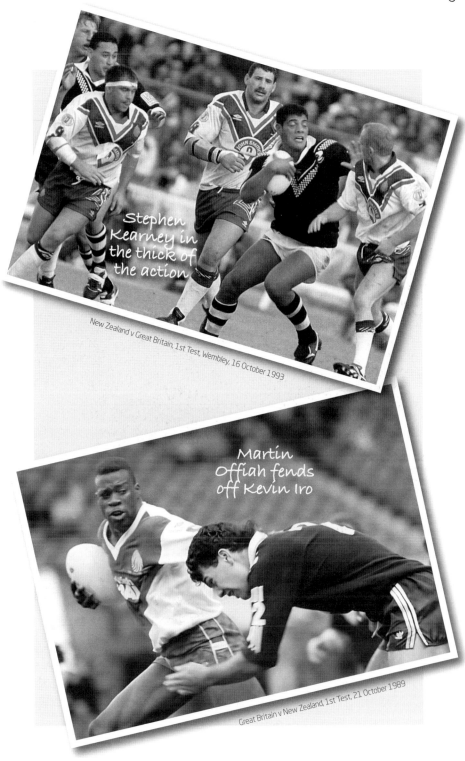

Stephen Kearney in the thick of the action

New Zealand v Great Britain, 1st Test, Wembley, 16 October 1993

Martin Offiah fends off Kevin Iro

Great Britain v New Zealand, 1st Test, 21 October 1989

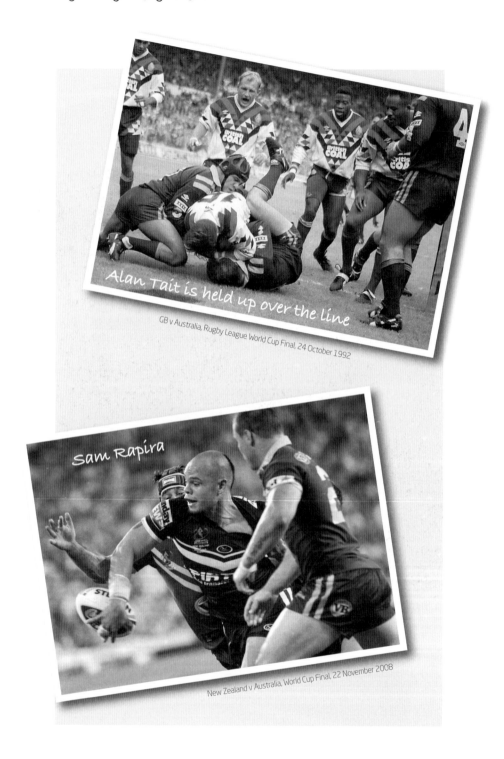

Alan Tait is held up over the line

GB v Australia, Rugby League World Cup Final, 24 October 1992

Sam Rapira

New Zealand v Australia, World Cup Final, 22 November 2008

Henry Paul lifts the 2000 Challenge Cup alongside his brother Robbie after Bradford defeated Leeds at Murrayfield

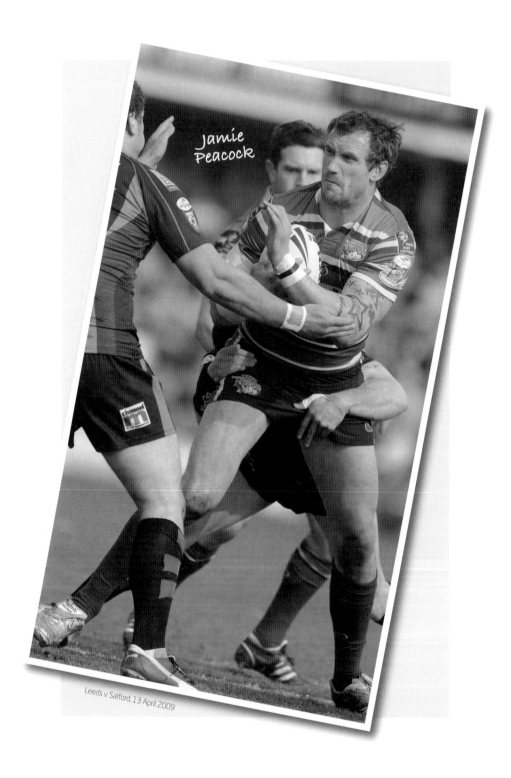

Jamie Peacock

Leeds v Salford, 13 April 2009

'Spot the difference'

Twins Kevin (9) and Bob (7) Beardmore playing for Castleford, Castleford v Leeds, Yorkshire Cup 1st Round, 16 September 1984

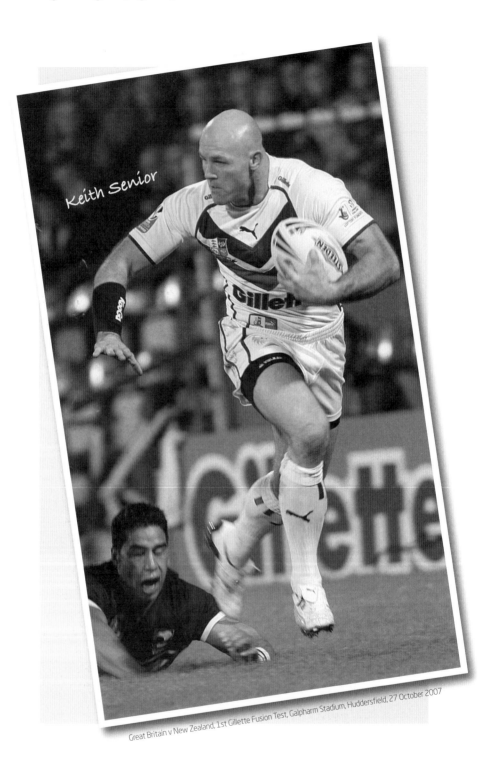

Keith Senior

Great Britain v New Zealand, 1st Gillette Fusion Test, Galpharm Stadium, Huddersfield, 27 October 2007

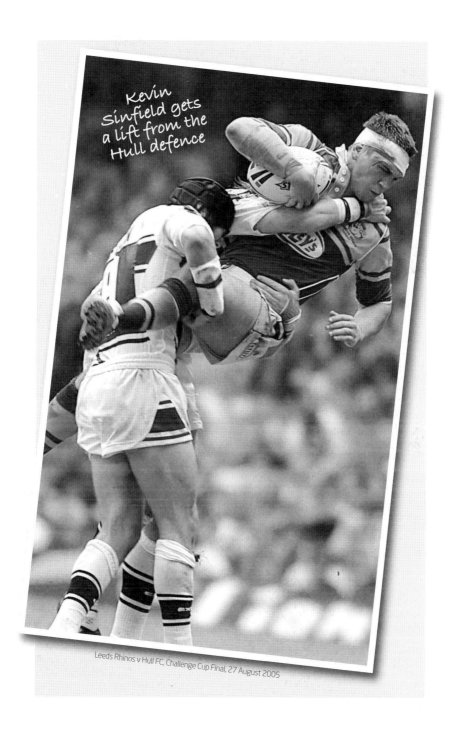

Kevin Sinfield gets a lift from the Hull defence

Leeds Rhinos v Hull FC, Challenge Cup Final, 27 August 2005

Kelvin Skerrett powers past Stuart Spruce for a try

Wigan 20 v Widnes 14, Rugby League Challenge Cup Final, 1993

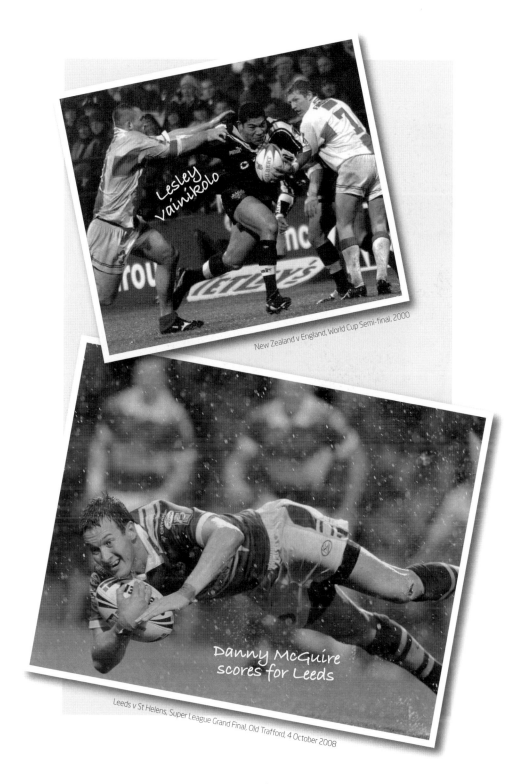

Lesley
Vainikolo

New Zealand v England, World Cup Semi-final, 2000

Danny McGuire
scores for Leeds

Leeds v St Helens, Super League Grand Final, Old Trafford, 4 October 2008

Great Britain v New Zealand, 1st Gillette Fusion Test, Galpharm Stadium, Huddersfield, 27 October 2007

Craig Horne

Dewsbury v Keighley, 23 July 2000

Paul White

3 June 2007

Henry Paul in action for Wakefield

Wakefield v Featherstone, 2 January 1994

Garry Schofield holds off Martin Dermott to score

Wigan 26 v Leeds 16, 1994 Rugby League Challenge Cup Final, 30 April 1994